# FUN FACTS

## Ripley's Believe It or Not! Kids

### & SILLY STORIES

# THE MANE EVENT!

**RIPLEY PUBLISHING**

a Jim Pattison Company

# What's Inside?

**Wacky Puzzles!**
PAGE 116

**Silly Creations!**
PAGE 35

**A Tasty Recipe!**
PAGE 60

消火栓

**Buggy Facts!**

PAGE 118

**Crazy Q&As!**

PAGE 38

**Super Stories!**

PAGE 18

# CHECK THIS! OUT!

## REALLY?
Underwater pumpkin carving

## NO WAY!
Scuba cat

## CUTE
Airport therapy pig

## CRAZY
Mountain slide

## WOW!
Hamdog

Bonedigger the lion at the G.W. Exotic Animal Park in Wynnewood, Oklahoma, has a pack of doggy friends! Dachshunds Milo, Bullet, and Angel have comforted the disabled lion since he was just a cub.

# Beast Friends

After seeing how well the dogs got along with Bonedigger, their handler, John Reinke, introduced them to other big cats.

Play-Doh was originally used as wallpaper cleaner.

# REINVENTING THE WHEEL!

A 15-year-old boy from Farmington, Maine, invented earmuffs in 1873!

In ancient Southeast Asia, the incense clock was used to track time.

Play-Doh was originally used as wallpaper cleaner.

# REINVENTING THE WHEEL!

A 15-year-old boy from Farmington, Maine, invented earmuffs in 1873!

In ancient Southeast Asia, the incense clock was used to track time.

In 1902, George Darby of England patented a fire alarm made from butter—it sounded an alarm when the butter melted.

In 1943, engineer Dick James invented the Slinky toy . . .

Rich Olson of Seattle, Washington, created an alarm clock that shreds your money if you fail to get up to turn it off!

. . . by accident while making springs for US warships.

# Under the BIG TOP

Find all 16 terms hidden in the circus tent! Make sure to look up, down, backward, across, and diagonally!

acrobat

tightrope

applause

bumper cars

fun house

animals

sideshow

balloon

unicycle

candy

clowns

magician

strongman

big top

arena

trapeze

```
a  p  p  l  a  u  s  e  j  t  j  c  u  j  x  n  m  t  t  f
q  h  f  r  u  l  i  s  h  d  a  n  d  s  u  a  g  a  z  u
e  s  u  o  h  l  d  n  l  n  q  i  g  x  d  m  a  y  j  n
m  i  y  p  y  e  e  e  d  a  o  w  o  r  e  g  r  d  a  h
k  m  y  o  u  r  s  y  t  x  m  e  n  z  h  n  e  h  j  o
h  k  a  t  n  d  h  s  g  s  v  i  e  p  k  o  n  q  l  u
m  v  r  g  v  z  o  p  z  w  m  p  n  j  w  r  a  b  u  s
b  d  s  i  i  k  w  n  b  l  a  q  e  a  n  t  x  y  h  e
o  m  j  b  j  c  y  t  x  r  b  o  z  i  t  s  r  h  q  p
l  q  y  t  r  u  i  b  t  x  e  t  a  m  b  j  m  p  q  e
t  a  b  o  r  c  a  a  s  a  f  u  n  e  r  e  n  n  k  e
n  s  w  w  j  m  s  x  n  i  q  q  m  g  p  t  u  o  a  f
l  k  c  r  w  a  g  o  f  g  a  w  b  o  v  n  b  o  u  r
h  f  p  l  y  n  t  v  j  u  s  z  r  a  i  y  u  l  y  y
p  o  r  w  o  w  w  d  b  s  f  t  r  c  z  t  e  l  t  x
t  n  k  n  j  w  c  c  n  o  h  l  y  p  t  c  g  a  e  c
b  y  m  q  e  r  n  r  p  g  b  c  l  v  x  a  e  b  a  n
z  j  n  x  l  f  m  s  i  w  l  g  b  g  t  g  f  r  h  m
k  x  i  i  b  j  b  t  k  e  l  u  j  b  d  x  l  q  z  z
v  u  u  w  j  a  z  b  s  r  a  c  r  e  p  m  u  b  v  w
```

**Want to see how you did?**
Turn to pages 136-138 for the solutions!

Bee-lieve it or not, bees come in colors other than yellow and black!

# Orchid Bees

They are found mostly in Central and South America, have extremely long tongues, and don't live in a hive.

Orchid bees can be blue, purple, red, orange, and green!

# Creepy Crawlies

Mosquitoes are attracted to smelly feet!

A praying mantis is the only insect that can turn its head.

Earthworms breathe through their skin.

Approximately 2,000 silkworm cocoons are needed to produce one pound of silk.

The Hercules beetle can carry up to 850 times its own weight on its back!

Caterpillars have more muscles than humans.

One of the heaviest insects is New Zealand's giant weta, which can weigh more than a mouse.

# Pig Tale

LiLou is the first known therapy pig to work in a US airport. She helps calm stressed travelers at the San Francisco International Airport.

# Defying Gravity

Congrats!

Don't be a chicken!

Duck! Here comes a plane!

A sheep, a duck, and a rooster were the first passengers on a hot air balloon.

The wingspan of a Boeing 747 is longer than the Wright brothers' first flight.

Kites were used to deliver letters during the American Civil War.

Miles Daisher of Twin Falls, Idaho, invented "skyaking"—skydiving while sitting in a kayak and landing on water.

Spider-Man has a hyphen in his name so that people don't confuse him with Superman.

Super Facts

# Hidden Heroes

Find all 16 superheroes hidden in disguise! Make sure to look up, down, backward, across, and diagonally!

Spider-Man

Iron Man

Superman

Captain America

Green Arrow

Flash

Batman

Thor

Wolverine

Aquaman

Hulk

Professor X

Wonder Woman

Doctor Strange

Wasp

Black Panther

BONUS! Find the hidden villain in this puzzle. Write the villain's name here:

_____ !

g a n c g l e b g o i i k i n g m g o a
q s q a f m a n n a m o w r e d n o w t
b u o v m f l a s m x h w a h c d s x g
y g w h l t h e j o k e r o s o q i o n
m o f c j o a l o x b h w d c p x q f o
e a v r a o h b x g o e r t g e w a l s
n q i q g p y s w a g e o p a c i h a a
c u w u s y t j i c a r l r b f i a s h
l a h a m u p a r i s r r o s r r a h c
h m j m s k p a i t i p o f o e o n q h
h a e s w e l e r n n n i e i p n h n a
x n c f o r s a r o a a k s o q m o t m
b h e l l h n j a m h m a s p r a q n e
m b e y v g e r a o a h e o i x n i p r
a s w x e h i o f i i n n r b i g n k x
n i j a r w w s n s h d i x i l d i l i
h e s p i d e r m a n a w r w c u a u f
w b i e n s b e r o w w r l s p a n h l
l a w l e j o b l a c k p a n t h e r o
k t g e w o r r a n e e r g e r h f d b

**Want to see how you did?**
Turn to pages 136-138 for the solutions!

The least weasel is the smallest carnivore in the world.

# Weasel Out!

Some weasels become all white in the winter.

Before killing prey, weasels will bob back and forth and hop in a dance, and scientists aren't sure why.

They must eat constantly to provide enough energy, since their bodies don't store fat.

Though weasels can dig their own burrows, they also take over other animals' burrows, sometimes even taking over termite hills.

Weasels save leftover food, digging little underground stashes near their den entrances.

23

Since 2010, the nonprofit organization Washed Ashore has removed 17 tons of waste from Oregon beaches—turning plastic pollution into art!

# All Washed Up!

# All about Jellies...

Scientists have merged jelly and feline DNA to create glow-in-the-dark cats!

Jellies eat fish, shrimp, crabs, and tiny plants.

Jellies existed before dinosaurs.

# Under the Sea

Today _____ and I went scuba diving in the ocean near _____ !
**person** **noun**

The weather was _____ , not a _____ in the sky. Our guide
**adjective** **noun**

_____ us into our _____ and then we were on our way! The
**verb ending in -ed** **noun**

water was a little _____ , but we could see so many _____ .
**adjective** **noun**

Besides all the _____ fish, we saw _____ , _____ ,
**adjective** **plural noun** **plural noun**

and even a _____ _____ ! I thought it would be loud
**adjective** **singular noun**

underwater, but it was so _____ . I was a little _____ when
**adjective** **verb ending in -ed**

_____ swam by, though. Our guide made sure we _____ away
**noun** **verb ending in -ed**

from the _____ so we stayed safe. I hope we can do this again soon.
**noun**

# The BIG EYE-dea

Dolphins sleep with one eye open.

Horses have the largest eyes of any land mammal.

EYE am the champion!

Polar bears have a third eyelid that helps them filter out UV light.

Each eye of the tarsier is bigger than its brain, and they are so large that they can't move in their sockets!

EYE see you (and you and you...)!

Flies have two eyes, but they contain more than 4,000 smaller eye lenses!

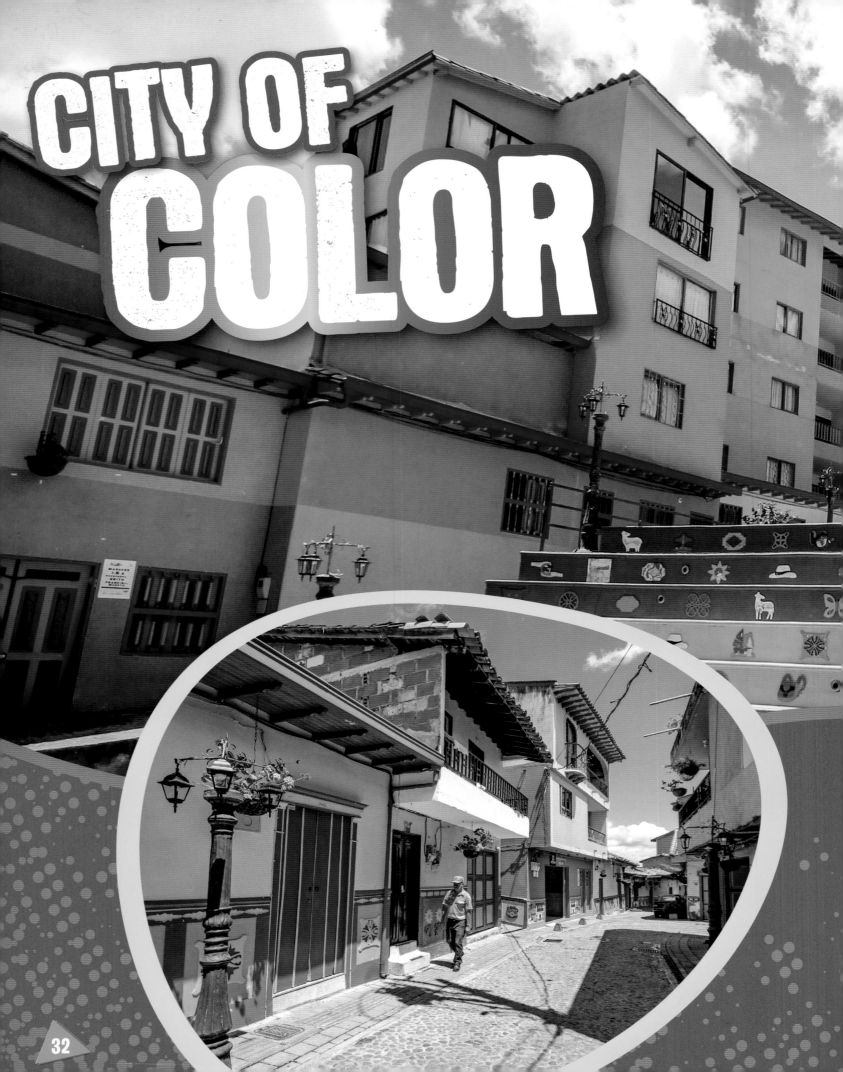

# CITY OF COLOR

Stunning color dazzles the eye in the small town of Guatapé, Colombia! Most of this town—from walls and doors to balconies and steps—is painted in bright, vibrant colors!

Food curators Miss Cakehead and the Tattooed Bakers once created a life-size unicorn cake! The tasteful creature was filled with rainbow-colored cake layers.

# Hungry for More

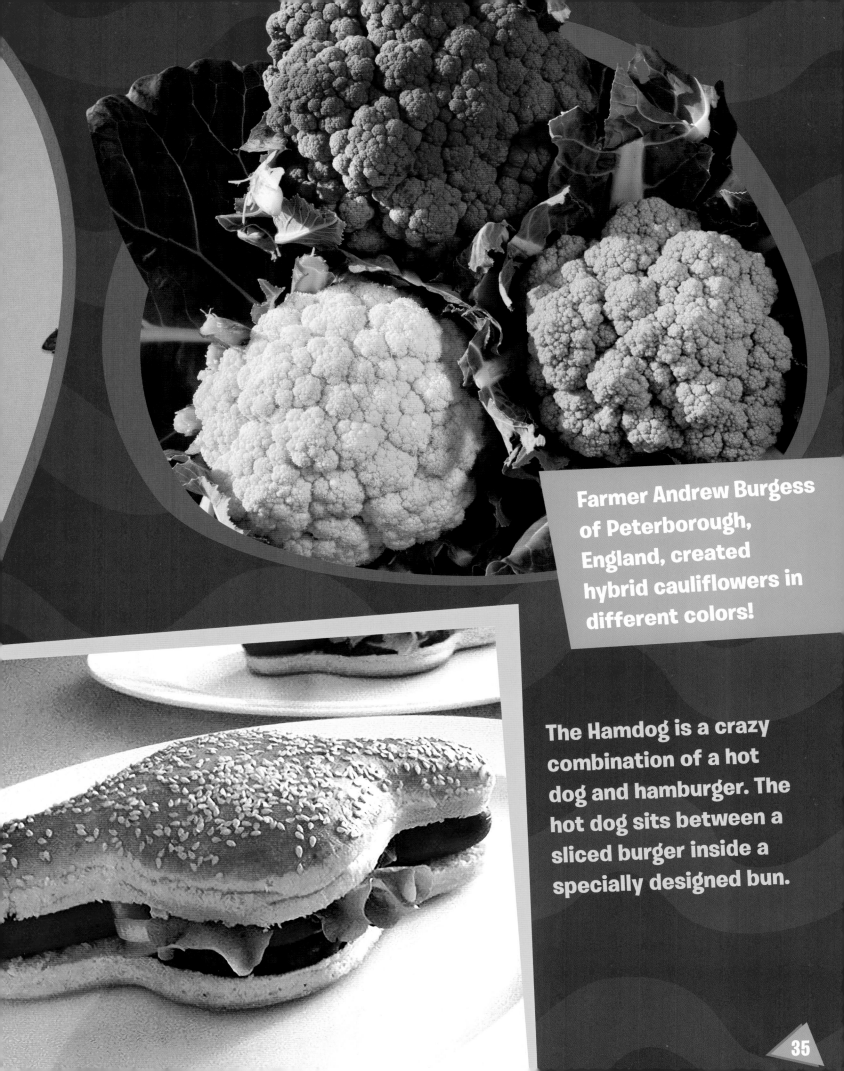

Farmer Andrew Burgess of Peterborough, England, created hybrid cauliflowers in different colors!

The Hamdog is a crazy combination of a hot dog and hamburger. The hot dog sits between a sliced burger inside a specially designed bun.

# Strange Slices

Pizza is enjoyed all across the globe, but it's not always prepared in familiar ways. Check out how these countries like to top their pies!

**Costa Rica**
coconut
shrimp
pineapple

Brazil
green peas
quail eggs
raisins

Japan
mayonnaise
corn
bacon

It's served cold!

Russia
mackerel
sardines
salmon

India
pickled ginger
sheep
tofu

Sweden
peanuts
bananas
curry powder

Color in these popular pizza toppings from around the world!

37

# One Foot Wander

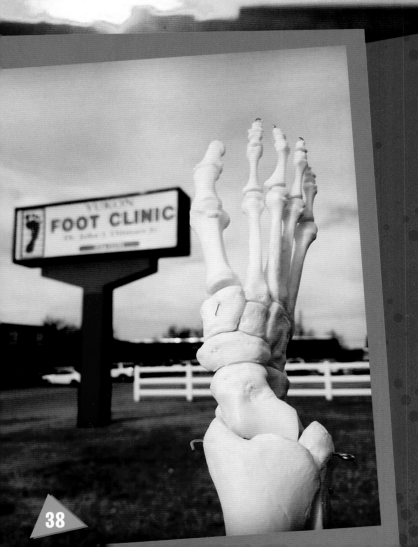

After being diagnosed with cancer, Kristi Loyall of Oklahoma was forced to amputate her right foot—but decided to keep it! She started the Instagram account @onefootwander, showing her cleaned, whitened foot posing in funny situations.

FOOT CLINIC

## Ripley's Asks...

**We had a chat with Kristi and her funny bone.**

**Q:** What gave you the idea to keep your foot after the amputation?

**A:** When my doctor told me amputation would be the best option, the first thing I asked was if I could have my foot back. One of my coping mechanisms is to make a joke out of things, so that's what I was trying to do, and then I realized I really did want my foot back.

**Q:** Did you name your foot? If so, what's its name?

**A:** Sometimes I call it Footzilla, but the actual name I came up with is Achilles.

**Q:** What kind of reactions do you get when you are out with your foot?

**A:** I think most people assume it's fake when they see it. No one has ever really commented on it while I was taking photos. One time when I was at a drive-thru, the cashier saw my best friend holding it and said, "I like your foot," and I thought, "Haha, if only you knew."

# Photo Shoot

While in Bandipur Tiger Reserve in Karnataka, India, a wildlife photographer caught this monkey checking himself out in a car mirror—sometimes even kissing his own reflection!

Meet Demyte, or "Little Spot," the winner of Ramygala, Lithuania's goat beauty contest.

A diver at Australia's Great Barrier Reef captured this image that appears to show his friend being eaten alive by a massive Napoleon wrasse! (It's actually an optical illusion.)

Believe it or not, April 17 is Bat Appreciation Day!

Despite their name, sun bears are nocturnal.

Kodiak bear cubs weigh less than a pound when born, but grow to be one of the largest bears in the world.

# Bear with Us!

Sloth bears will put their mouths over insect nests and suck up bugs through a gap in their front teeth.

Giant pandas have an extra large bone on their paws specifically for holding bamboo.

Black bears can be black, brown, cinnamon, blond, blue-gray, or white.

Polar bears are the only carnivorous bear species; all others are omnivores.

# Cute but Deadly

Every year, moose actually attack more people than bears.

The bite of a tiny blue-ringed octopus can kill an adult human within minutes.

The adorable slow loris secretes poison from its elbows.

The adult male platypus has a venomous pointed spur above the heel of each hind leg.

Pufferfish poison is very potent and can easily kill by paralyzing the diaphragm, causing suffocation.

When disturbed, the flightless cassowary bird of Australia and New Guinea is capable of using its large claws to disembowel its attacker.

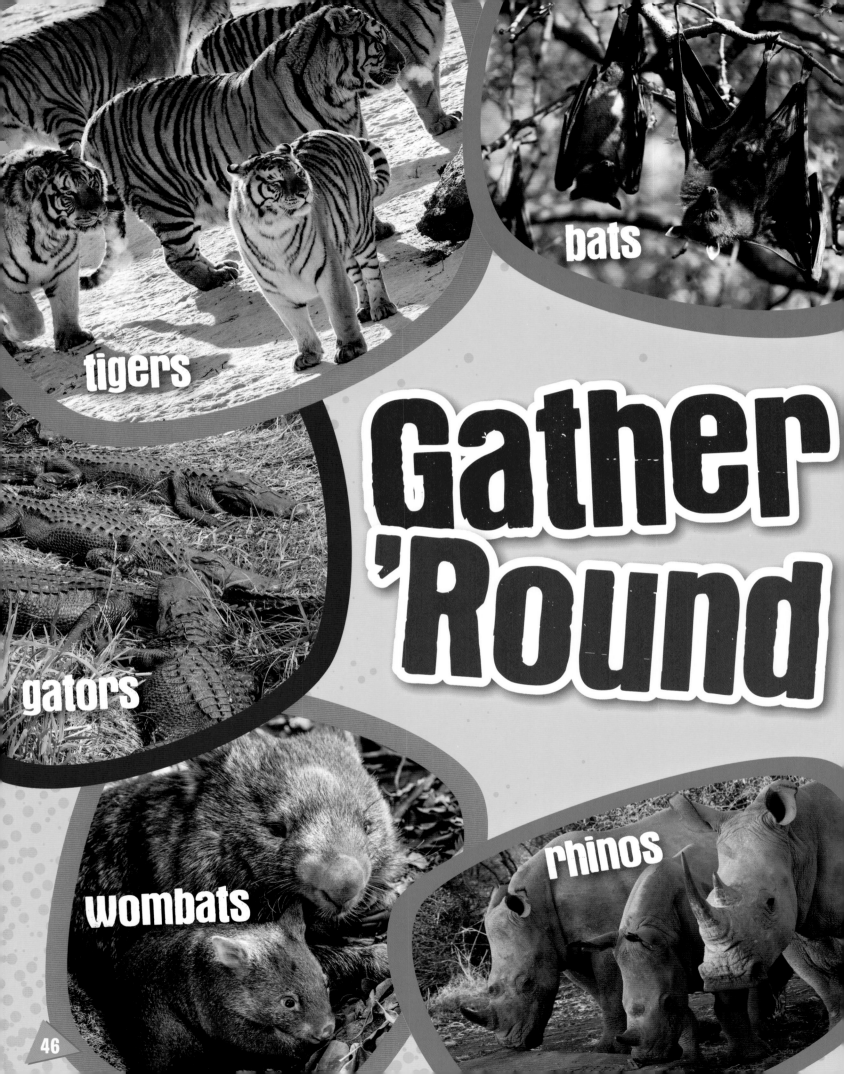

tigers

bats

gators

# Gather 'Round

wombats

rhinos

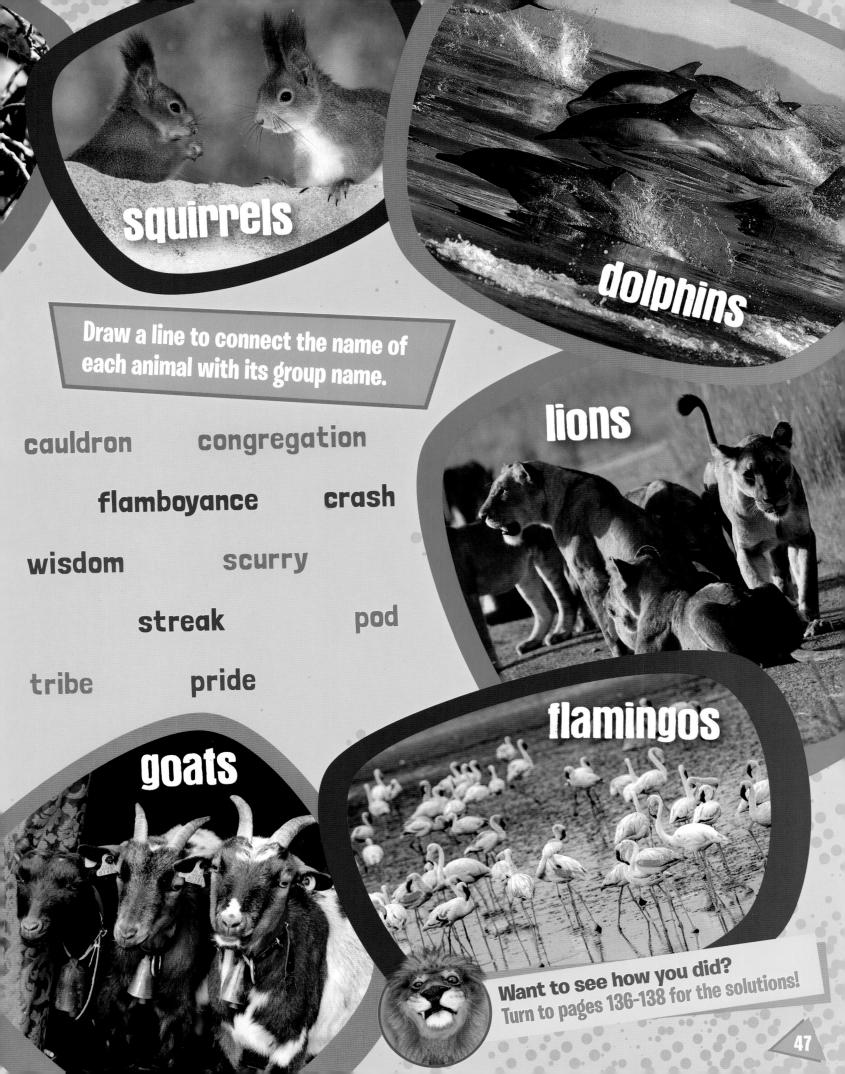

squirrels

dolphins

Draw a line to connect the name of each animal with its group name.

cauldron          congregation

flamboyance          crash

wisdom          scurry

streak          pod

tribe          pride

lions

flamingos

goats

Want to see how you did?
Turn to pages 136–138 for the solutions!

# It's Going Down

Looking up from below Trifonov's balloon

Austrian pilot Ivan Trifonov successfully landed a hot-air balloon in the 675 feet deep Mamet Cave in Croatia.

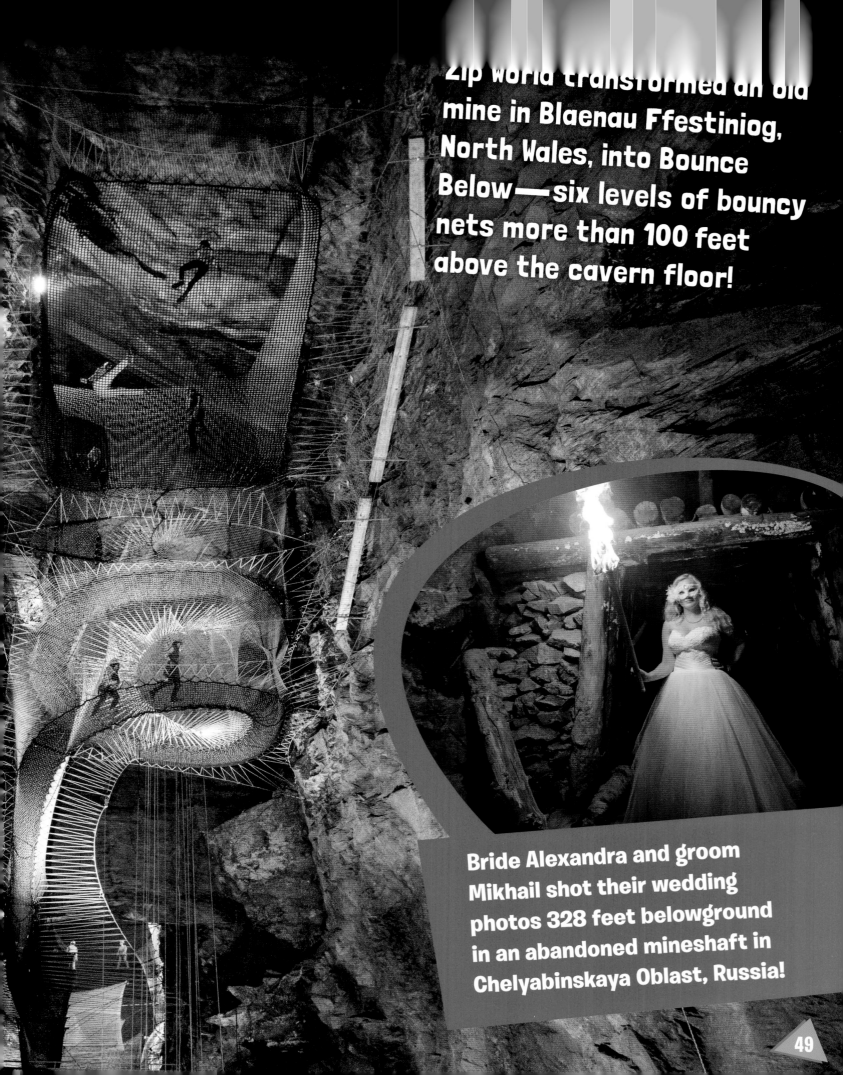

Zip world transformed an old mine in Blaenau Ffestiniog, North Wales, into Bounce Below—six levels of bouncy nets more than 100 feet above the cavern floor!

Bride Alexandra and groom Mikhail shot their wedding photos 328 feet belowground in an abandoned mineshaft in Chelyabinskaya Oblast, Russia!

Sianagh Gallagher dominates the rock climbing wall despite being born with no arm, collarbone, or shoulder blade on the left side of her body.

# Rock the WALL

The York, England, native is captain of the Great Britain Paraclimbing Team, whose members are all differently abled athletes.

# Mountain Slide

Rodelbahn alpine roller coasters race through thousands of feet of the Swiss Alps. Riders travel in a wheeled toboggan while controlling their own speed with a cart-mounted brake and must slow themselves down to keep from toppling over on turns.

Follow the slides to find out which team makes it to the bottom without taking a detour!

FINISH

Want to see how you did?
Turn to pages 136-138 for the solutions!

# Sporty Animals

I want to be like Hawkeye!

Hawkeye the cat went on more than 20 underwater trips after her owner, Gene Alba of Redding, California, built her a custom scuba suit!

This silly seal pup hopped onto Karen Mikado's kayak multiple times as she was rowing in British Columbia, Canada. The animal visited several other boats too, something their tour guide said they had never seen before!

A team of dogs in South Africa have been trained to parachute and rappel from helicopters in order to help find kand stop animal poachers!

# LITTLE SHOP of Cheeses

**An unknown artist called Anonymouse opened secret mice-sized shops hidden in the city of Malmö, Sweden!**

Although the artist is a mystery, these tiny shops for mice offer nuts, cheese, and a cozy atmosphere.

Terry Taylor from Essex, England, feeds wild robins, putting a worm between his lips for them to nab.

# For the Birds

Made from the spit of the cave-dwelling swiftlet bird, these nests are used to make soup and can cost thousands of dollars per pound!

# PB & Worm Cookies

## Stuff you need:

- ½ pound earthworms
- 1 cup peanut butter
- 1 cup sugar
- 1 teaspoon vanilla
- 1 egg
- 1 cup flour

1. Boil earthworms for 10 minutes and drain.
2. Mix all ingredients together.
3. Divide dough into balls and place 1 inch apart on an ungreased cookie sheet.
4. Bake 12 to 15 minutes at 350°F.

Feeling a little grossed out? Substitute creepy crawlies with candy! Use 12 Tootsie Rolls to replace the worms. Roll out candies to resemble worms. Skipping step 1, prepare as instructed, and while cookies are still hot, place your candy worms on top!

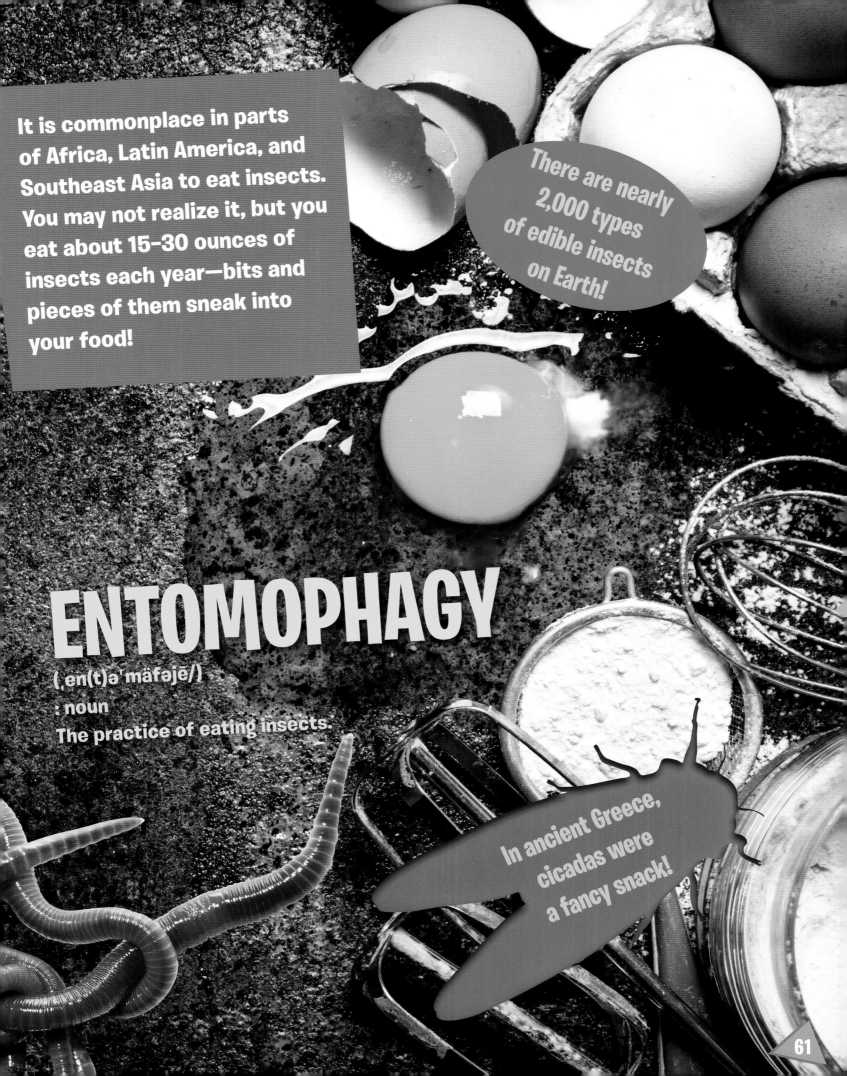

It is commonplace in parts of Africa, Latin America, and Southeast Asia to eat insects. You may not realize it, but you eat about 15-30 ounces of insects each year—bits and pieces of them sneak into your food!

There are nearly 2,000 types of edible insects on Earth!

# ENTOMOPHAGY

(ˌen(t)əˈmäfəjē/)

: noun

The practice of eating insects.

In ancient Greece, cicadas were a fancy snack!

# Don't Blink!

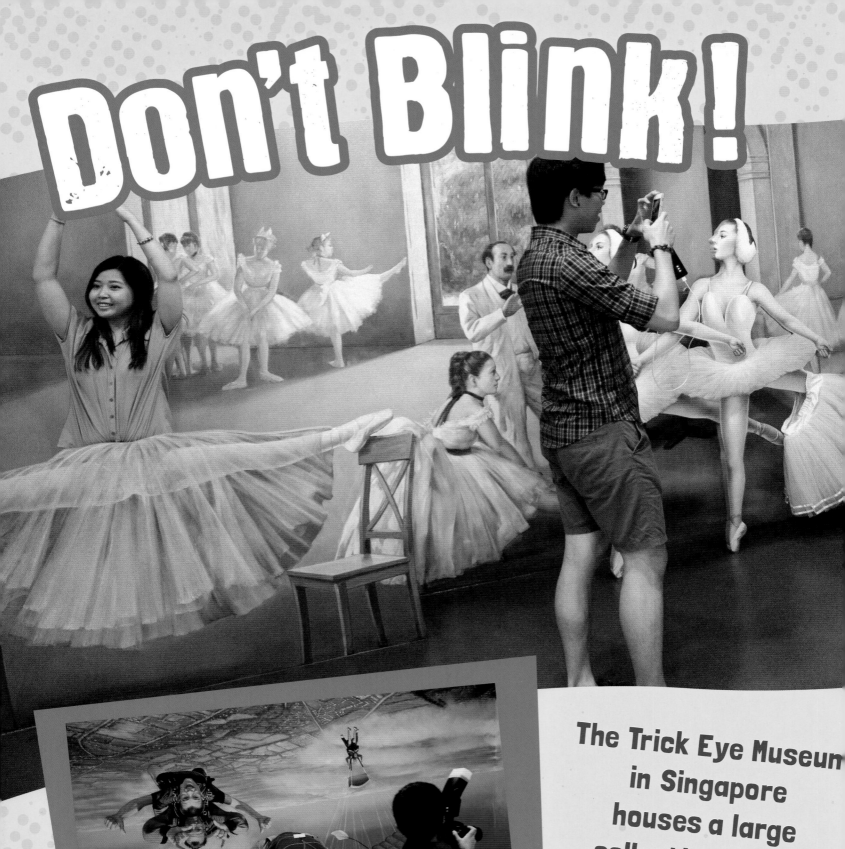

The Trick Eye Museum in Singapore houses a large collection of 3-D art for people to create fun optical illusions.

The Moken people of Southeast Asia, who have deep-dived for food for centuries, have underwater vision twice as sharp as Europeans.

# Chinese New Year

Did you know? A Chinese New Year tradition is to give red envelopes filled with money.

YUE HWA
CHINESE PRODUCTS

Each year is associated with a zodiac animal:

| | | | |
|---|---|---|---|
| Rat | Rabbit | Horse | Rooster |
| Ox | Dragon | Goat | Dog |
| Tiger | Snake | Monkey | Pig |

Chinese New Year, also known as the Spring Festival, is the most important holiday in China. Between January and February, families come together to rest, eat, celebrate a year of hard work, and wish for a lucky and prosperous new year.

65

# Year of the Rooster

To celebrate 2017, the year of the rooster, a hotel in Shenyang, China, displayed an 11.8-foot-tall rooster sculpture made from 330 pounds of butter!

Citizens and tourists flocked to a beauty contest for chickens on January 22, 2017, in Foshan, Guangdong Province, China.

In December 2016, a barber shop gave one kid a cluck-tastic hairstyle to match the upcoming year of the rooster.

# Year-End

Can you find the seven differences between the two scenes? Color in the differences.

BONUS: Spot the balloon in this picture.

68

# Round-up

How many smaller words can you make out of the letters in the words below? Words must have four letters or more.

Want to see how you did? Turn to pages 136-138 for the solutions!

## HAPPY NEW YEAR

_____     _____

_____     _____

_____     _____

_____     _____

_____     _____

_____     _____

# Lovey Dovey

Foxie the chimp lives in a sanctuary in Washington State and always carries a toy troll wherever she goes.

This heart-shaped swarm of bees was spotted by Alan Hollis while on a walk through the Malvern Hills in Worcestershire, England.

In August 2016, Kelin Flanagan and Spencer Taubner's engagement photo shoot in Banff National Park, Alberta, Canada, was photobombed by a ground squirrel!

# What's in the Water?

Alien-like feather stars are marine invertebrates with arms that have feathery fringes used for swimming.

The cute ribbon seal (*Histriophoca fasciata*) is patterned with four white bands and can be found in the icy waters off Russia's southern coast and north of Korea and Japan.

The blobfish might not look so flabby and gross when at home, since deep sea pressure gives their bodies structural support.

# Ice World

Fill in the blanks with the correct Antarctic or Arctic animal. Then order the numbered letters to reveal the secret message!

① I have thick, white fur and strong paws to catch seals.

__ __ __ __ __ __ __
21      7         3

② I'm a bird that can't fly, but I can swim!

__ __ __ __ __
12   9   15    16

③ I'm known as the unicorn of the sea.

__ __ __ __ __
18   14   1   10    4

④ I have two long tusks and a whole lot of blubber.

__ __ __ __
22   5    8   19

⑤ I help Santa pull his sleigh!

__ __ __ __ __ __
   17   20   13

⑥ I'm a small, white whale with a big head.

__ __ __ __ __
2   6     11

## SECRET MESSAGE:

__ __ __ __ __ __ __ __ __ __ __ __ __ __ __ __ __ __ __ __ __ __
1   2   3   4   5   6   7   8   9   10   11   12   13   14   15   16   17   18   19   20   21   22

# Help the orca calf find her way back to her pod!

**Want to see how you did?**
Turn to pages 136-138 for the solutions!

# Nutty Nature

Penguin droppings, or guano, can be seen from space! Satellite images show the stark contrast between the icy landscape of Antarctica and the dark color of penguin poop.

When in danger, armadillo lizards curl into a ball—just like an armadillo!

A species of fruit fly has an ant image on each wing. It is thought that the insect markings confuse the fly's main predator, a jumping spider.

An electric eel is not an eel at all, but a type of knifefish.

Despite its name, the bearcat is not closely related to bears or cats.

Hippopotamus literally means "river horse" in Greek.

The elephant shrew is more closely related to elephants than shrews.

Groundhogs are also known as woodchucks or whistlepigs.

# What's in a Name?

Wait... What?

A group of frogs is called an army.

Early explorers in Antarctica classified penguins as fish.

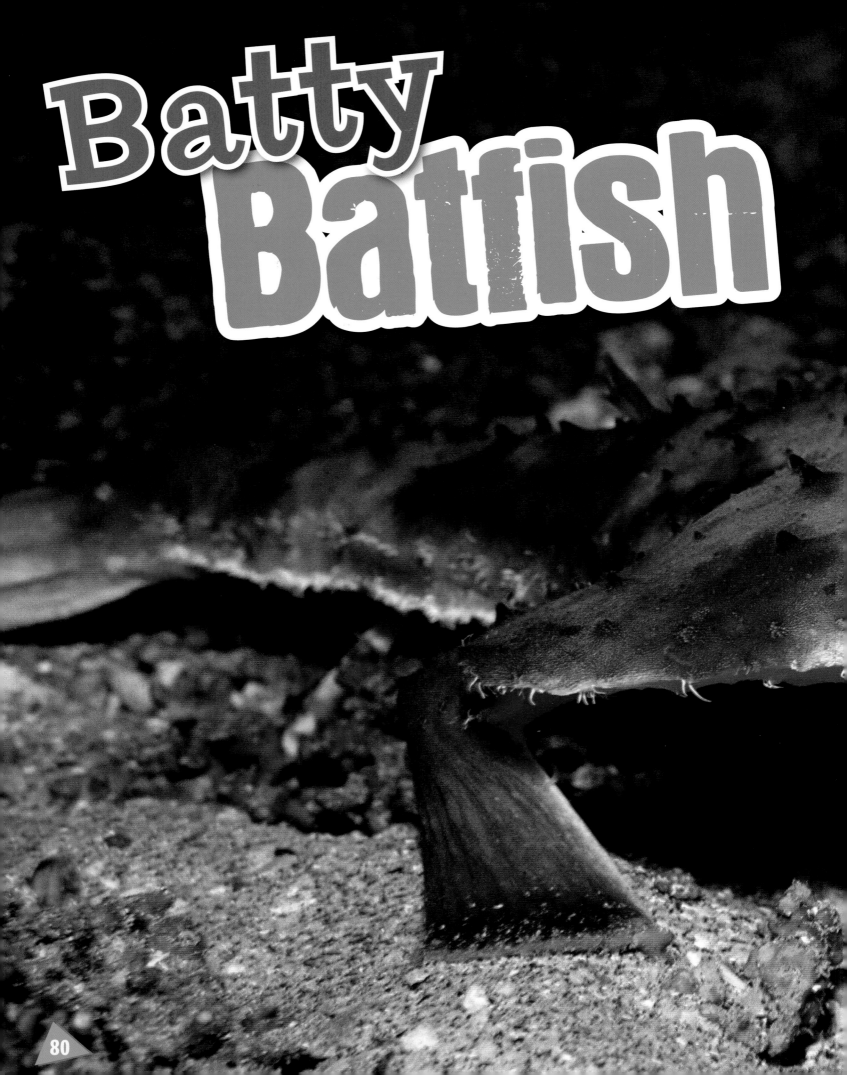

# Batty Batfish

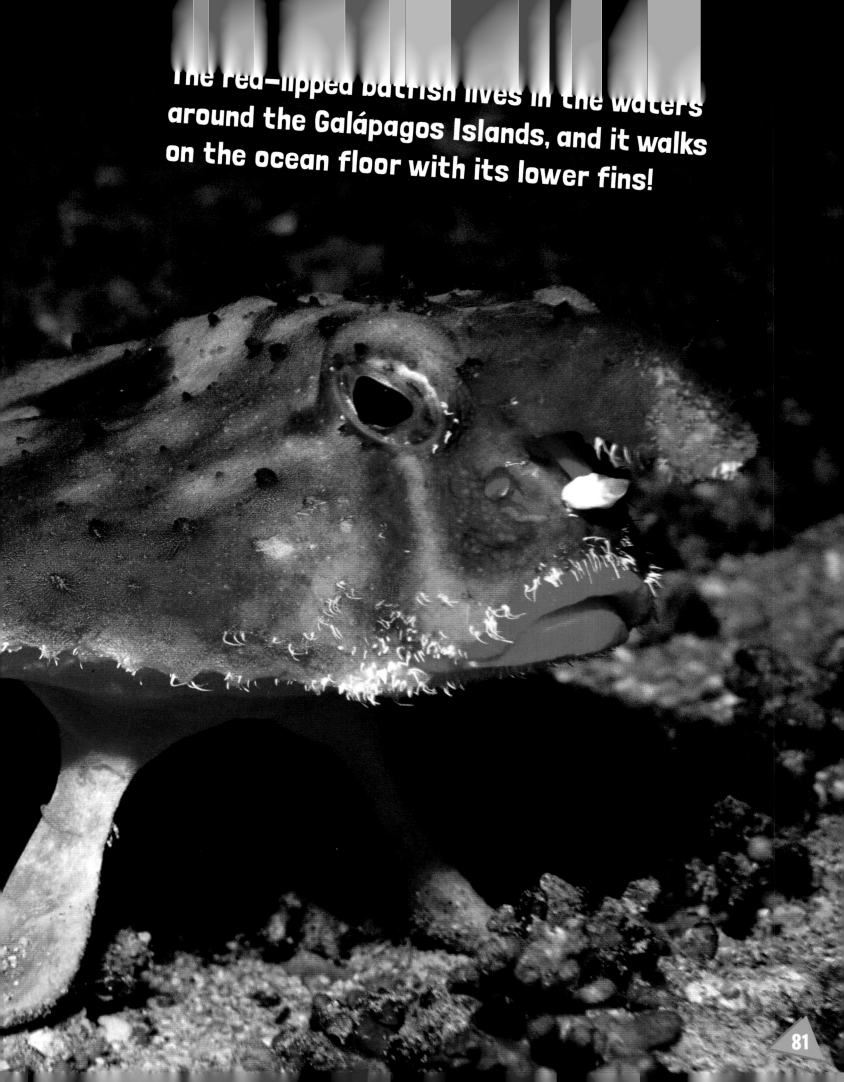

The red-lipped batfish lives in the waters around the Galápagos Islands, and it walks on the ocean floor with its lower fins!

Singapore-based artist Cynthia Delaney Suwito knits with instant noodles!

# Knitting Noodles

Cynthia sees instant noodles as something that people find comfort in because they are quick and easy. To help people slow down, she takes what is "instant" and makes it time-consuming.

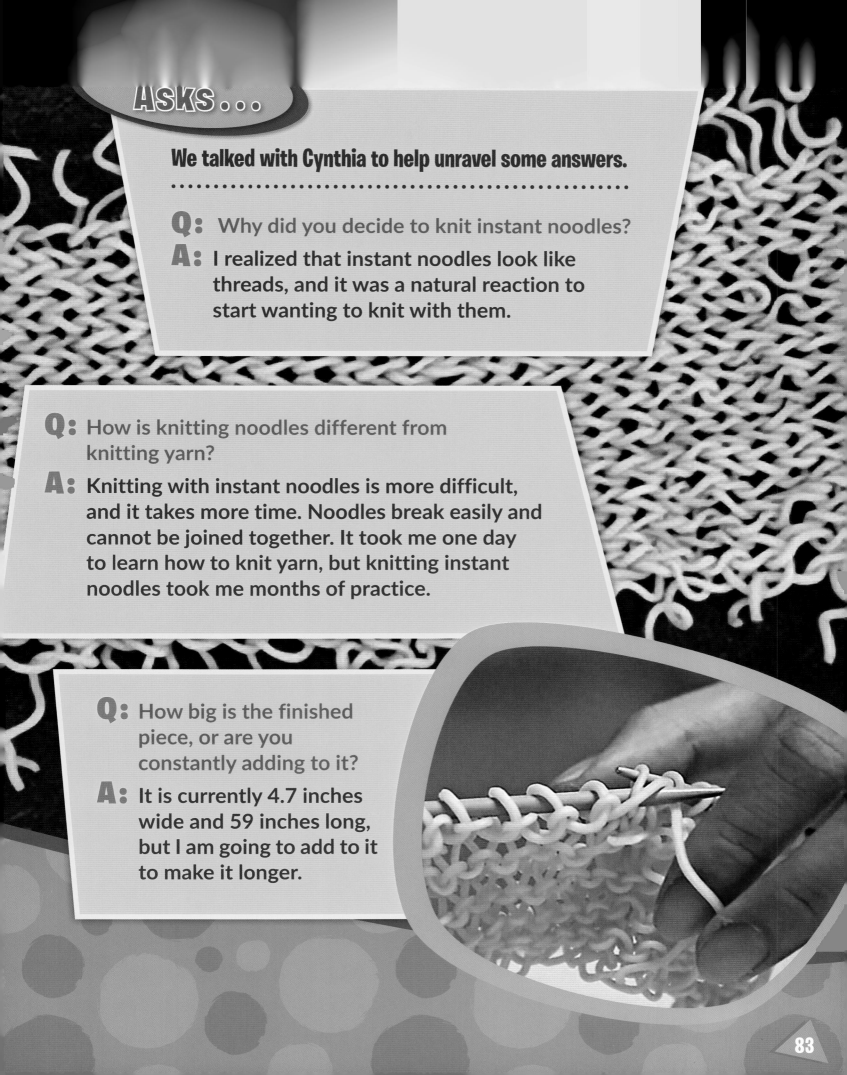

**ASKS...**

We talked with Cynthia to help unravel some answers.

**Q:** Why did you decide to knit instant noodles?

**A:** I realized that instant noodles look like threads, and it was a natural reaction to start wanting to knit with them.

**Q:** How is knitting noodles different from knitting yarn?

**A:** Knitting with instant noodles is more difficult, and it takes more time. Noodles break easily and cannot be joined together. It took me one day to learn how to knit yarn, but knitting instant noodles took me months of practice.

**Q:** How big is the finished piece, or are you constantly adding to it?

**A:** It is currently 4.7 inches wide and 59 inches long, but I am going to add to it to make it longer.

American cotton candy is called "candyfloss" in the UK and India, "fairy floss" in Australia and Finland, and "old ladies' hair" in Greece!

Ranch dressing contains the same ingredient used in sunscreen and paint to make it appear whiter.

# Dining In?

Threads of cotton candy are thinner than a human hair.

Scientists can turn peanut butter into diamonds!

Native Alaskans invented a type of ice cream made of reindeer fat, seal oil, fresh snow, and berries.

Astronauts Neil Armstrong and Buzz Aldrin ate hot dogs on their mission to the moon!

Throwing away food is illegal in Seattle, Washington.

You can buy eel-flavored ice cream in Japan.

Dry weather conditions in 2014 made it difficult for wild hedgehogs in the UK to get ready for hibernation.

# Hedgehog

I'm looking pretty sharp today!

To help the small animals, British home improvement store B&Q teamed up with the Wildlife Aid Foundation to create this hedgehog-sized "drive-thru"!

MENU
SNAILS
SLUGS
MEALWORMS
CENTIPEDES

OPEN

TODAY'S
SPECIALS

FRESH
BEETLES

DRIVE THROUGH

# Drive-Thru

It's filled with yummy bugs for the prickly creatures to eat!

# Desert DOTS

Connect the dots to see what desert animals are in the oasis.

START

88

In December 2016, it snowed in the Sahara Desert for the first time in 37 years!

START

What do you call a camel with no humps?

Humphrey!

Want to see how you did?
Turn to pages 136-138 for the solutions!

Visitors to Gumeracha, Australia, can climb the world's biggest rocking horse at the Toy Factory!

Barbie's actual full name is Barbara Millicent Roberts.

There are 43 quintillion possible Rubik's cube combinations.

# Toyland

Using more than three million bricks, former *Top Gear* host James May and the BBC built a LEGO house in 2009! It even featured a flushable toilet.

The first version of Minecraft was created in just six days.

All cows in Minecraft are female, since they can all give out milk.

# Minecraft

One of Minecraft's stranger native species, the creeper, actually began as a coding error.

If Minecraft were real, one Minecraft block in real life would equal 1 m³. That means the Minecraft world is bigger than some planets.

The creator's personal Minecraft avatar is the only game resident who drops an apple when he dies.

The Enderman language is actually English in reverse (and at a lower pitch).

One in every 10,000 times you play the game, its introductory menu will flash a misspelling of the title, reversing the "E" and the "C" to read "Minceraft."

93

Instant ramen noodles were the first noodles ever consumed in space.

SPACE RAM - MISO
100 mls hot water *5 min
5215          SFSL007

RAM - TONKOTSU
ls hot water *5 min
SFSL002

# Spaced Out

A sample of Sir Isaac Newton's apple tree was sent into space to "defy" gravity.

"Astronauts" come from America, while space explorers from Russia are called "cosmonauts."

# Snack Attack

Doritos were invented at Disneyland.

According to two similar stories, pink lemonade was created by the circus!

Carrots were originally purple.

Legend has it that pretzels were first made by Italian monks in the 7th century.

The word "companion" is derived from Latin *com*, "together," and *panis*, "bread."

Cheese is the most stolen food in the world.

$$$

Roman soldiers were partially paid in salt, known as *solarium argentum*, which is how we get the word "salary."

In ancient Egypt, onions symbolized eternity, and Egyptians even buried Pharaohs with onions, including King Ramses IV, who was entombed with onions in his eye sockets.

When chili peppers were introduced to Japan, people stuck them in their shoes to warm their toes!

# Kooky Kiwis

Kiwi birds are only found in New Zealand and are the national symbol of the count[r]

About the size of a chicken, kiwis are flightless birds with a long beak.

They got their name from the sound of their calls, making "kee-wee, kee-wee" noises.

Unlike other birds, kiwi chicks are already covered in feathers as soon as they hatch.

"Kiwi" is a nickname for people from New Zealand.

Kiwi fruit was named after the kiwi bird because they are both small, brown, and furry.

Kiwi fruits are actually native to China.

The brown fuzz on kiwi fruit is actually edible!

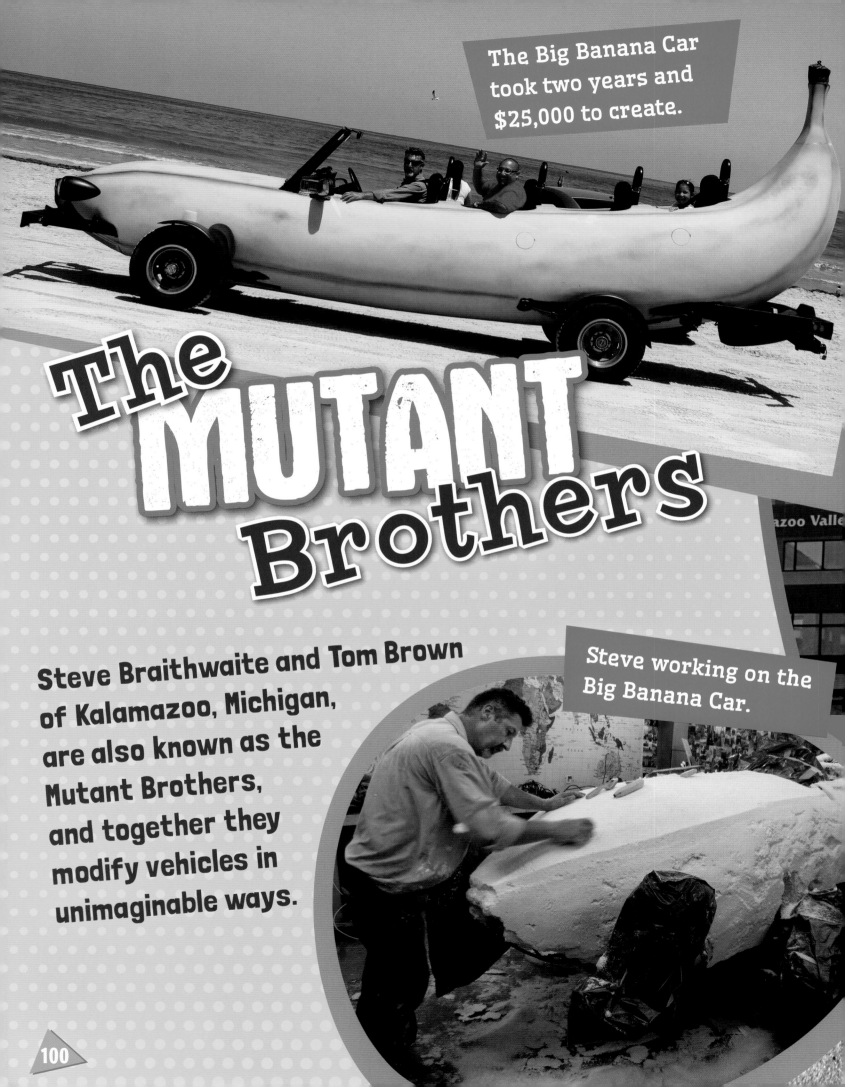

The Big Banana Car took two years and $25,000 to create.

# The MUTANT Brothers

Steve working on the Big Banana Car.

Steve Braithwaite and Tom Brown of Kalamazoo, Michigan, are also known as the Mutant Brothers, and together they modify vehicles in unimaginable ways.

The Mutant Brothers also created the Topsy Turvy Bus. The final product weighs 14,700 pounds and is 13 feet high.

# Blast from the Past

When she met Mark Antony, Cleopatra is said to have arrived on a golden barge rowed by oars made of silver, while attendants dressed as cupids fanned her.

Pope Benedict IX was the youngest pope ever, between 12 and 20 years old when he started his rule.

In 2012, a couple invited Queen Elizabeth II to their wedding as a joke, and she turned up.

Alexander Graham Bell, the inventor of the telephone, wanted people to say "Ahoy" when answering the phone.

Albert Einstein was once asked to be the president of Israel. He turned it down.

Thomas Jefferson invented the swivel chair.

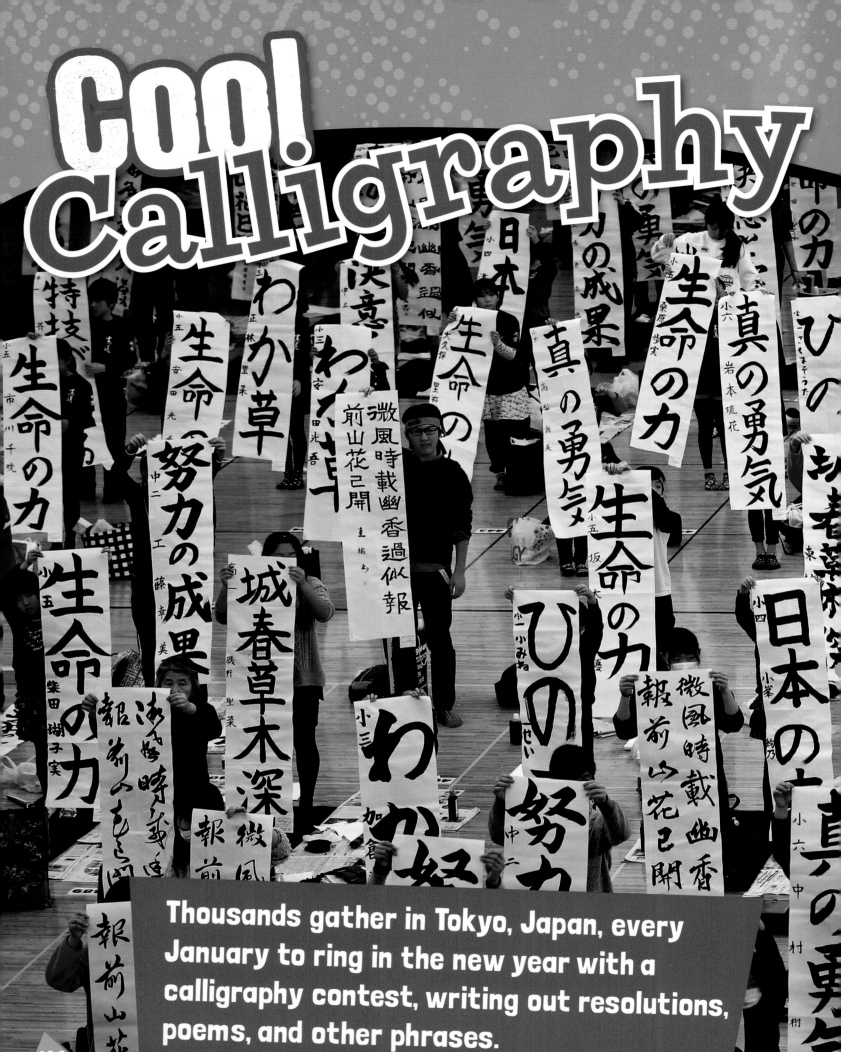

# Cool Calligraphy

Thousands gather in Tokyo, Japan, every January to ring in the new year with a calligraphy contest, writing out resolutions, poems, and other phrases.

# Can You Kanji?

These two characters, or symbols, mean "Happy New Year" in kanji!

## KANJI

(ˌkän-(ˈ)jē)

: noun

A Japanese writing system with symbols that represent whole ideas rather than individual sounds.

賀春

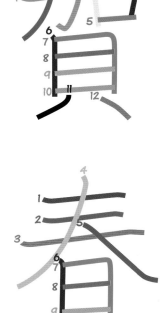

In Japan, hanko, or stamps, are used in place of signatures. Artists can customize their hanko by having their last name or a favorite word or phrase carved on their seal.

Follow the numbered steps to the left and try your hand at writing this Japanese New Year's greeting in kanji. Then, sign it with your own hanko design in the red square!

# Jumbo Jackets

When temperatures plummeted, Wildlife SOS Elephant Conservation and Care Center in Mathura, India, knitted jumbo jackets for their rescued elephants.

# Flying High

Follow the path to find out which numbered net Zazel lands in.

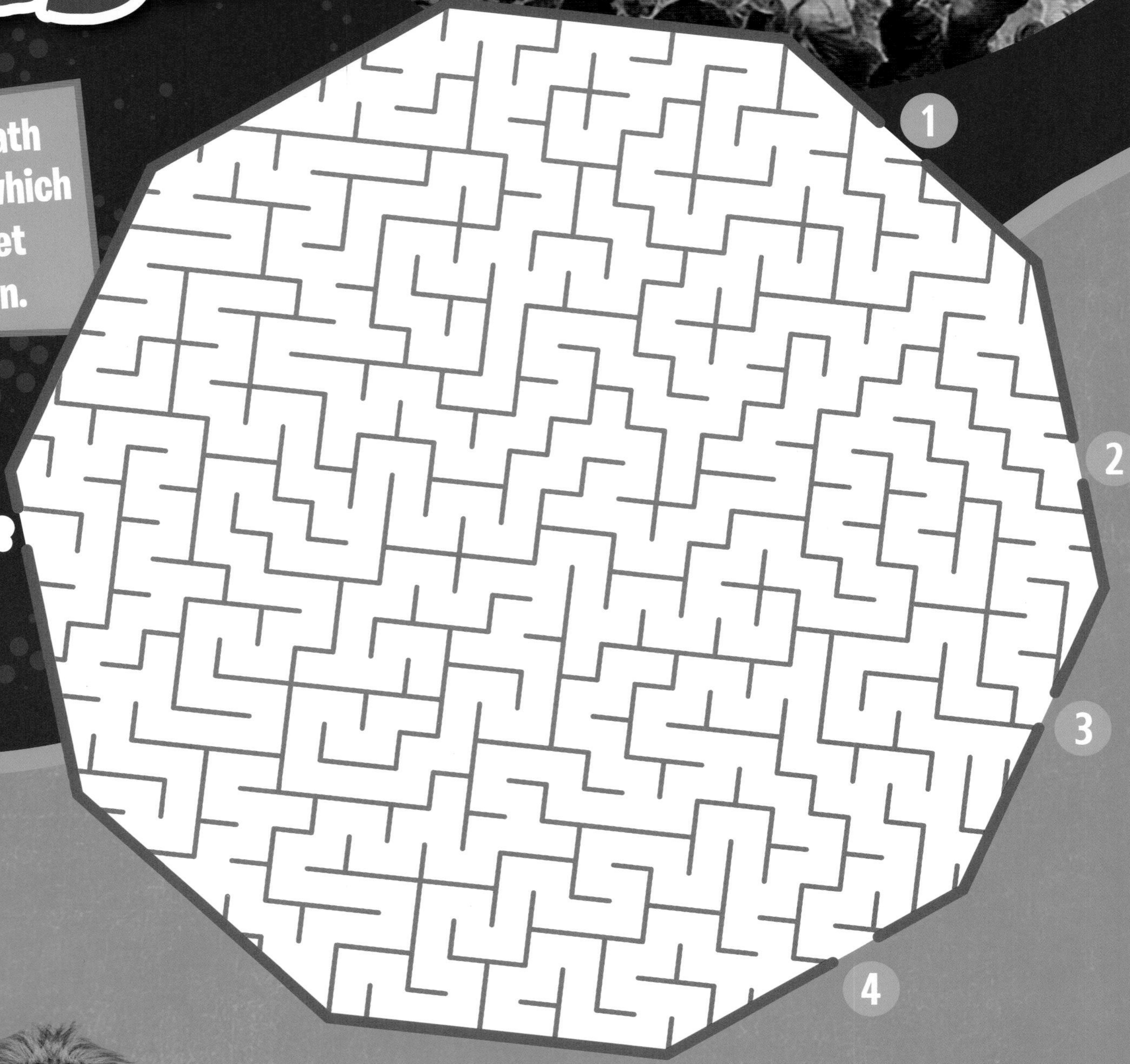

START HERE

1

2

3

4

**Want to see how you did?**
Turn to pages 136-138 for the solutions!

The first recorded human cannonball was a 14-year-old girl—acrobat Rosa "Zazel" Richter—who was shot 30 feet into the air in London, England, in 1877.

**POSSIBLE**

**3 letters**
net
air
fly

**4 letters**
girl
high
bold
bang
exit

**5 letters**
human
Zazel
brave
stunt
first

**6 letters**
safety
steady
launch

**7 letters**
acrobat
ability
strange
pioneer

**8 letters**
possible
athletic
dramatic
momentum
dizzying

**9 letters**
daredevil
dangerous
entertain

**10 letters**
cannonball

Using the word bank, write the words on the criss-cross grid. We've placed one word to get you started!

The Royal Children's Hospital in Melbourne, Australia, built a permanent meerkat enclosure. The animals' high level of activity and social interaction make them perfect pals for children receiving treatment and in recovery.

# Meerkat Medics

British artist Cléon Daniel constructed a banana–shaped pool table.

# Puzzling Pursuits

London artist Yoni Alter created a 19-piece 3-D puzzle that looks like an Air Jordan shoe.

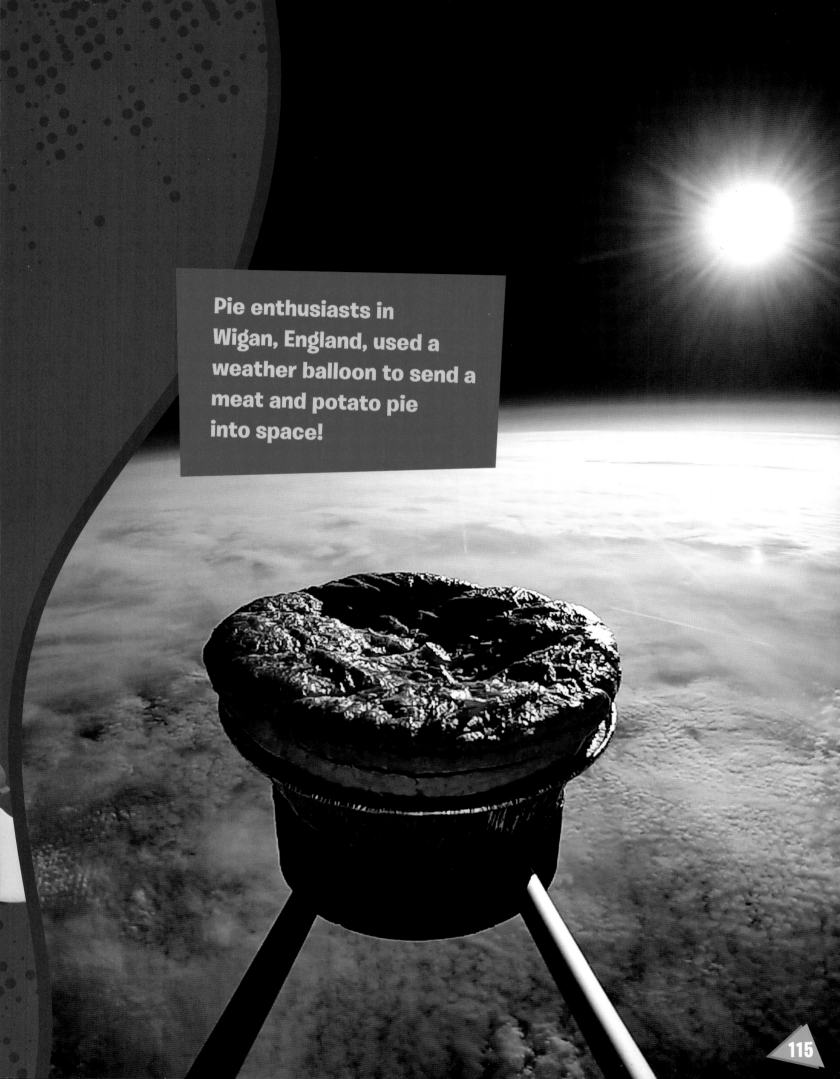

Pie enthusiasts in Wigan, England, used a weather balloon to send a meat and potato pie into space!

# Manhole Art

Manhole covers in Japan feature kawaii, or cute, designs!

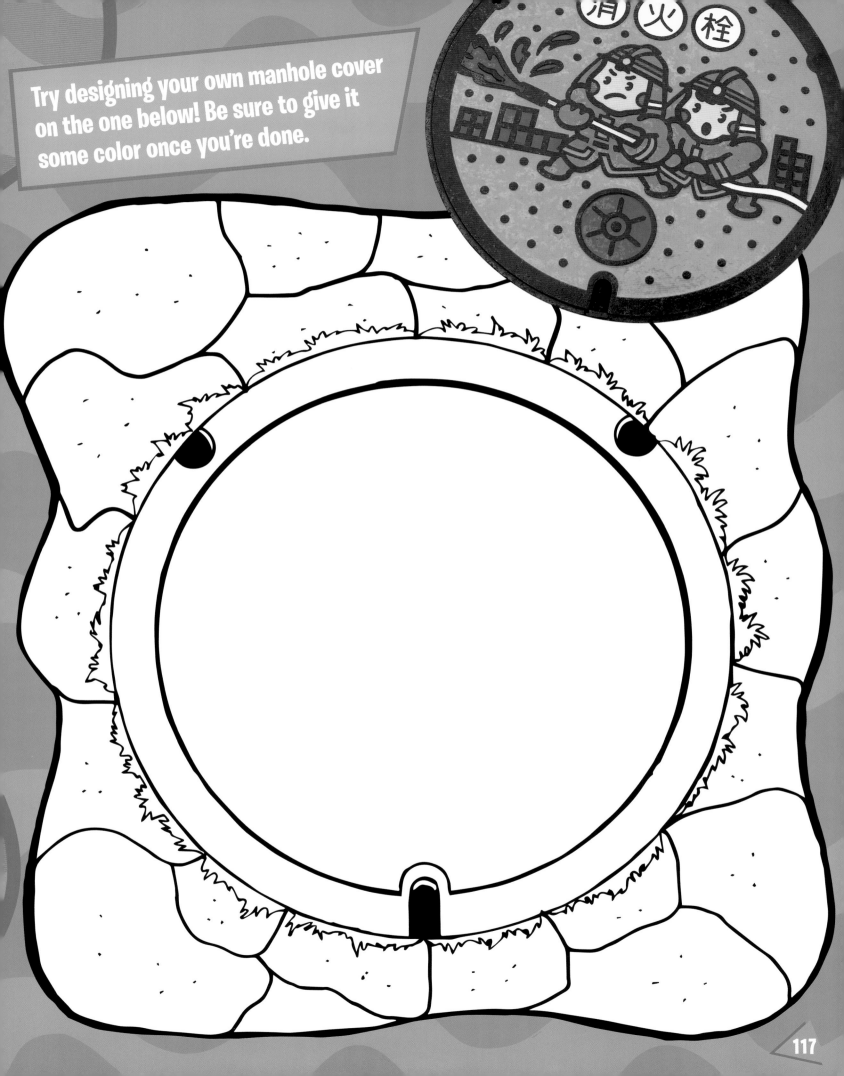

Try designing your own manhole cover on the one below! Be sure to give it some color once you're done.

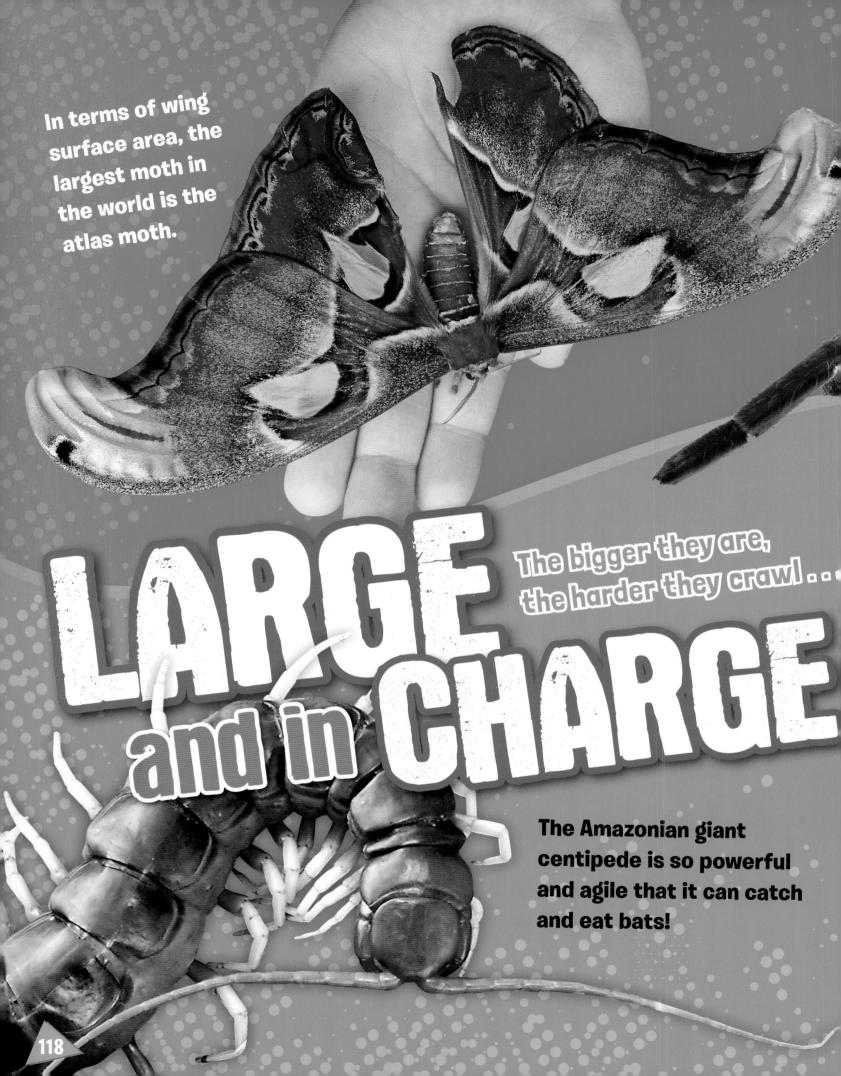

In terms of wing surface area, the largest moth in the world is the atlas moth.

# LARGE and in CHARGE

The bigger they are, the harder they crawl . . .

The Amazonian giant centipede is so powerful and agile that it can catch and eat bats!

The goliath birdeater tarantula of South America is the biggest spider in the world!

Its legs can span up to 1 foot wide!

Found in South America, the titan beetle is a giant! Their mouthparts, or mandibles, are so strong they can snap wooden pencils in half!

# In Deep

**Fisherman Mick Brown hooked a hefty pike fish that was in the middle of eating a 4-foot-long eel!**

The pearlfish takes shelter inside a sea cucumber's butt.

The *Cymothoa exigua* isopod invades a fish's mouth, causes its tongue to fall out, and then camps out where the tongue used to be.

Luke Skywalker's lightsaber flew into space aboard the space shuttle *Discovery*.

While filming *Star Wars* in the Pacific Northwest, Chewbacca actor Peter Mayhew had bodyguards to protect him from bigfoot hunters.

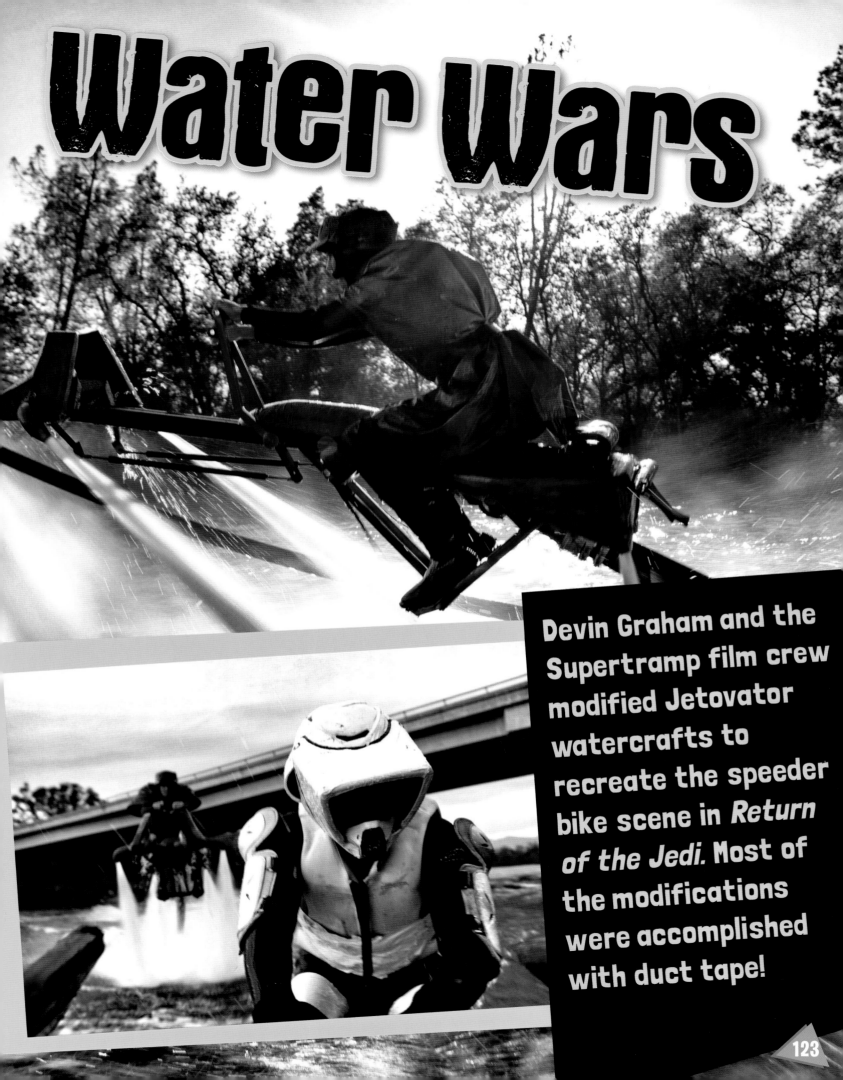

# Water Wars

Devin Graham and the Supertramp film crew modified Jetovator watercrafts to recreate the speeder bike scene in *Return of the Jedi.* Most of the modifications were accomplished with duct tape!

123

The Kayashima train station in Osaka, Japan, has a huge camphor tree growing in the middle of it, which officials believe is about 700 years old!

# At Face Value

A building in Shanghai, China, was turned into a giant strawberry cake in November 2016.

# Home Sweet What?

Artist Cheri Pann and her husband Gonzalo Duran have turned their house in Venice, California, into a giant mosaic of tile, figurines, and even coffee mugs and silverware!

The mysterious Margate Shell Grotto in England is actually an underground passageway lined with thousands of seashells!

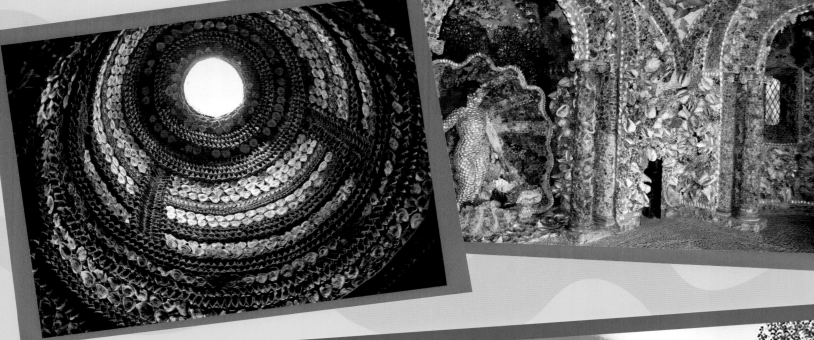

John Milkovisch covered his house in Houston, Texas, with more than 50,000 aluminum cans!

More than 171 million Americans celebrated Halloween in 2016.

Jack-o'-lanterns originated in Ireland, but since they didn't have access to pumpkins, they would carve turnips and rutabagas.

For Halloween 2016, some of our divers at the Ripley's Aquarium in Gatlinburg, Tennessee, carved pumpkins underwater in our Shark Lagoon!

# Trick or Treat Yourself

At many pumpkin festivals, people make huge pumpkin pyramids containing thousands of gourds that stretch up high into the air!

## GOURD
(gôrd, goord)

: noun
A gourd is a fleshy, typically large fruit with a hard skin, some varieties of which are edible.

# Halloween Fun!

Give this jack-o'-lantern a scary face!

Germany's Ludwigsburg Castle hosts an annual giant pumpkin boat race in the former royal palace's massive fountain!

Draw the rectangles in the correct order to reveal the spooky picture.

Want to see how you did?
Turn to pages 136-138 for the solutions!

**6**

**12**

**2**

**10**

**4**

**1**

**3**

**8**  TRICK OR

**11**

**5**

**9**

**7**

TREAT

TREAT

❶

❷

❸

❹

❺

❻

❼

❽

❾

❿

⓫

⓬

Karen Schoeve of Argyle, Texas, invited four horses into her home for a Thanksgiving meal of celery, carrots, and turkey-shaped Rice Krispie treats!

# Horsegiving

Snoopy the dog has appeared more than any other character as a balloon in the Macy's Thanksgiving Day Parade.

Believe it or not, female turkeys don't gobble.

# Like&Subscribe

The music video for Psy's "Gangnam Style" was so popular it broke YouTube's view counter, which had to be upgraded.

Twitter's bird is called Larry.

Oh?

Steve Jobs once called Google to tell them the yellow gradient in the second "O" of their logo

Every tweet Americans send is being archived by the Library of Congress.

Facebook is primarily blue because Mark Zuckerberg suffers from red-green color blindness.

Every day about 50 years' worth of content is uploaded on YouTube.

Google has a version of their site translated into the Klingon language from *Star Trek*.

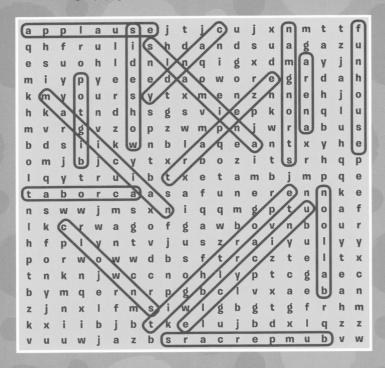

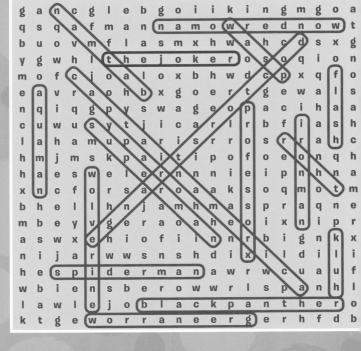

## Gather 'Round, page 46-47

**Streak = Tigers**

**Flamingos = Flamboyance**

**Bats = Cauldron**

**Goats = Tribe**

**Squirrels = Scurry**

**Rhinos = Crash**

**Dolphins = Pod**

**Wombats = Wisdom**

**Lions = Pride**

**Gators = Congregation**

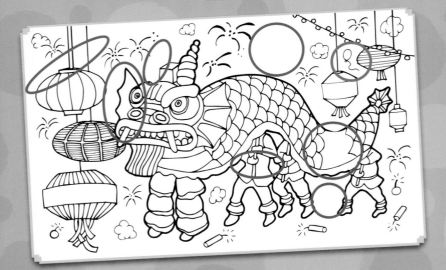

## HAPPY NEW YEAR

| | |
|---|---|
| Yawn | Pray |
| Hyper | Repay |
| Paper | Payer |
| Earn | Hyena |
| Near | Happen |
| Napper | Anyway |

1. I have thick, white fur and strong paws to catch seals.

2. I'm a bird that can't fly, but I can swim!

3. I'm known as the unicorn of the sea.

4. I have two long tusks and a whole lot of blubber.

5. I help Santa pull his sleigh!

6. I'm a small, white whale with a big head.

**P O L A R   B E A R**
21   7   3

**P E N G U I N**
12   9   15   16

**N A R W H A L**
18   14   1   10   4

**W A L R U S**
22   5   8   19

**R E I N D E E R**
17   20   13

**B E L U G A**
2   6   11

## SECRET MESSAGE:

**W E   A L L   L A U G H   A N D   R U N   I N   S N O W !**
2   3   4   5   6   7   8   9   10   11   12   13   14   15   16   17   18   19   20   21   22

Halloween Fun, page 131

Congrats!

# ABC's and 123's

Share some silliness and fun as little ones learn their ABC's and 123's. Filled with wacky, wonderful characters and sweet illustrations, they'll enjoy counting and saying their alphabet again and again!

# FUN FACTS & SILLY STORIES

Filled with wacky stories and colorful images of crazy animals, incredible talents, amazing people, and goofy events, readers will have a hard time putting these books down!

If you have a fun fact or a silly story, email it to us at bionresearch@ripleys.com

# OTHER TITLES IN THIS SERIES

aturing brand new Believe It or Not! ories, puzzles, and games, Ripley's ans are guaranteed to giggle and asp their way through these books!

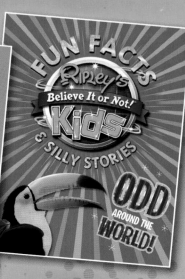

# ACKNOWLEDGMENTS

**FRONT COVER** © Andrew Lam/Shutterstock.com; **BACK COVER** (tr) © David Aleksandrowicz/Shutterstock.com, (bl) © Kawin K/Shutterstock.com; **IFC** © KengComp/Shutterstock.com; **2** (tl) © livcool/Shutterstock.com, (tr) blickwinkel/Alamy Stock Photo, (bl) © Tikhonov/Shutterstock.com; **2–3** (b) Courtesy of Mark Murray; **3** (tr) Kristi Loyall, @onefootwander, (br) © FUN FUN PHOTO/Shutterstock.com; **4** Barcroft USA; **5** (tr) © Steffen Foerster/Shutterstock.com, (b) © holbox/Shutterstock.com; **6** (t) © John99/Shutterstock.com, (cl) retales botijero via Getty Images, (br) © toon studio/Shutterstock.com; **7** (r) caia image/Alamy Stock Photo, (bl) © Jim Larson/Shutterstock.com, © vladwel/Shutterstock.com; **8** (tr) © YAKOBCHUK VIACHESLAV/Shutterstock.com, (b) © volodyar/Shutterstock.com; **9** © Kolonko/Shutterstock.com; **10–11** Nature Collection/Alamy Stock Photo; **12** (t) © Zety Akhzar/Shutterstock.com, (cr) © P Charnnarong/Shutterstock.com, (b) © Tikhonov/Shutterstock.com; **13** (tr) © Eric Isselee/Shutterstock.com, (cl) © suriya yapin/Shutterstock.com, (bl) © nokkaew/Shutterstock.com, (br) © Kim Howell/Shutterstock.com; **14–15** Courtesy of San Francisco International Airport; **16** (bl) © benjamas11/Shutterstock.com, (bc) © PhotoMediaGroup/Shutterstock.com, (br) © Lamyai/Shutterstock.com; **16–17** (t) © Robert Sarosiek/Shutterstock.com; **17** (br) © Gareth Cowlin/Shutterstock.com; **18** (tl) © StevePhotos/Shutterstock.com, (tr) © Irina Levitskaya/Shutterstock.com, (bl) © lacostique/Shutterstock.com, (bc) © Irina Levitskaya/Shutterstock.com; **18–19** © FUN FUN PHOTO/Shutterstock.com; **19** (tr) © SunshineVector/Shutterstock.com; **20** (tr) © Sarunyu L/Shutterstock.com, (b) © NoraVector/Shutterstock.com; **21** (tr) © Sarunyu L/Shutterstock.com; **22** (l) © Ian Maton/Shutterstock.com; **22–23** © wildphoto3/Shutterstock.com; **24–25** Washed Ashore/REX Shutterstock; **26–27** (bkg) © KengComp/Shutterstock.com, (b) © AnnaSimo/Shutterstock.com; **28–29** © Jag_cz/Shutterstock.com; **30** (tr) © Alla_Ri/Shutterstock.com, (bl) © Popsidoodle/Shutterstock.com; **31** (tl) © Don Mammoser/Shutterstock.com, (tr) © seafarer/Shutterstock.com, (br) © nattanan726/Shutterstock.com; **32–33** Jessica Devnani /Media Drum World/Caters News; **34** Tattooed Bakers www.tattooedbakers.com. Image by Baker and Maker; **35** (t) Bournemouth News/REX/Shutterstock, (bl)Courtesy of Mark Murray; **36–37** (bkg) © Artem Shadrin/Shutterstock.com; **38–39** Kristi Loyall, @onefootwander; **40** (tl) PALLAVI SARKAR/CATERS NEWS, (br) PETRAS MALUKAS/AFP/Getty Images; **41** GARY BRENNAND/ MEDIA DRUM WORLD/ CATERS NEWS; **42** (br) © SKARIDA/Shutterstock.com; **42–43** (bkg) © Zhou Eka/Shutterstock.com; **43** (bl) © AF studio/Shutterstock.com, (br) © Olga Lebedeva/Shutterstock.com; **44** (t) © Pictureguy/Shutterstock.com, (cr) © Teguh Tirtaputra/Shutterstock.com, (br) © Seregraff/Shutterstock.com; **45** (tl) © worldswildlifewonders/Shutterstock.com, (tr) © Boligolov Andrew/Shutterstock.com, (br) © Sanit Fuangnakhon/Shutterstock.com; **46** (tl) © Serjio74/Shutterstock.com, (tr) © tanaphongpict/Shutterstock.com, (cl) © Rudy Umans/Shutterstock.com, (bl) © Gekko Gallery/Shutterstock.com, (br) © Chris Price at PulseFoto/Shutterstock.com; **47** (tl) © geertweggen/Shutterstock.com, (tr) © Chase Dekker/Shutterstock.com, (cr) © Foto Mous/Shutterstock.com, (bl) © remore/Shutterstock.com, (br) © Anton_Ivanov/Shutterstock.com; **48–49** Zip World UK; **49** (cr) CATERS NEWS; **48** (l) Haron Markičević/MERCURY PRESS/CATERS NEWS; **50** Jim McAdam/Barcroft Media; **51** (tr) Jim McAdam/Barcroft Media, (bl) Barcroft Media; **52** Christoph Rueegg/Alamy Stock Photo; **53** (bl) Courtesy of Berghotel Oeschinensee Familie Wandfluh; **54** (br) © Volodymyr Krasyuk/Shutterstock.com; **54–55** (t) KAREN MIKADO/CATERS NEWS; **55** (b) Paramount Group Anti-Poaching and K9 Academy/CATERS NEWS; **56–57** (bkg, tr) Instagram @Anonymouse_mmx; **57** (br) Tommy Lindholm/Pacific Press/LightRocket via Getty Images; **58** (br) TERRY TAYLOR/MERCURY PRESS; **58–59** (bkg) TERRY TAYLOR/CATERS NEWS; **59** (tr) © sanooker_seven/Shutterstock.com, (b) © george photo cm/Shutterstock.com; **60** (tr) © viktor_kov/Shutterstock.com, (bl) © User:Bdevel, Tyler from Seattle, WA, Wikimedia Commons // CC-BY-SA 3.0.; **60–61** (bkg) © xtrekx/Shutterstock.com, (bc) © Tikhonov/Shutterstock.com; **61** (tr) © Artem Shadrin/Shutterstock.com, (br) © ArtHeart/Shutterstock.com; **62** (bl) REUTERS/Alamy Stock Photo; **62–63** (t) Xinhua/Alamy Stock Photo; **63** (r) Hemis/Alamy Stock Photo, (bl) Xinhua/Alamy Stock Photo; **64** (cl) © Chiradech Chotchuang/Shutterstock.com; **64–65** (bkg) Eugene Tang/Stockimo/Alamy Stock Photo; **66** VCG/VCG via Getty Images; **67** (t) VCG/VCG via Getty Images, (bl) Li Sixin/VCG; **70** (tl) DIANA GOODRICH/CATERS NEWS, (br) ALAN HOLLIS/MERCURY PRESS; **70–71** CATERS NEWS; **72** Els Van den Eijnden/Caters News; **73** (tr) Dr Carleton Ray via Getty Images, (br) © PavloArt Studio/Shutterstock.com; **74** (tr) © Jellis Vaes/Shutterstock.com; **76** Ashley Cooper/Alamy Stock Photo; **77** (tr) © reptiles4all/Shutterstock.com, (br) Peter Roosenschoon & Dubai Desert Conservation Reserve; **78** (tl) © Vladimir Wrangel/Shutterstock.com, (tr) © AppStock/Shutterstock.com, (b) © Christopher Robin Smith Photography/Shutterstock.com; **79** (tl) © ArtHeart/Shutterstock.com, (tr) © michelangeloop/Shutterstock.com, (bl) © Kawin K/Shutterstock.com, (br) © Firuz Salamzadeh/Shutterstock.com; **80–81** Mark Conlin/Alamy Stock Photo; **82–83** Cynthia Delaney Suwito; **84** (l) © Africa Studio/Shutterstock.com, (bl) © Hong Vo/Shutterstock.com, (br) © Robert-jihad/Shutterstock.com; **85** (tr) © michelaubryphoto/Shutterstock.com, (l) © M. Unal Ozmen/Shutterstock.com, (c) © musicman/Shutterstock.com, (br) NASA; **86–87** ASSOCIATED PRESS; **89** (cr) © David Aleksandrowicz/Shutterstock.com; **90** (t) De Klerk/Alamy Stock Photo, (br) © dnd_project/Shutterstock.com; **91** (tr) PA Images/Alamy Stock Photo, (br) James Boardman/Alamy Stock Photo; **92–93** Karwai Tang/WireImage; **94** (t) TONY MCNICOL/Alamy Stock Photo, (bl) © Art work/Shutterstock.com, (br) © Malinovskaya Yulia/Shutterstock.com; **95** (t) © Vadim Sadovski/Shutterstock.com, (b) © NASA images/Shutterstock.com; **96** (tl) © GMEVIPHOTO/Shutterstock.com, (tr) © Robert Grace/Shutterstock.com, (bl) © ArtCookStudio/Shutterstock.com, (br) © Dmitrij Skorobogatov/Shutterstock.com; **97** (tl) © Sean Locke Photography/Shutterstock.com, (tr) © COLOA Studio/Shutterstock.com, (cl) © LDWYTN/Shutterstock.com, (cr) © Naumov S/Shutterstock.com, (br) © cunaplus/Shutterstock.com, (br) © HelloRF Zcool/Shutterstock.com; **98–99** Travel Pictures/Alamy Stock Photo; **99** (tr) © KNEFEL/Shutterstock.com, (br) © Sarawut Aiemsinsuk/Shutterstock.com; **100** (t) Todd Lewis/Barcroft Cars, (br) Barcroft Cars; **101** (bkg) Todd Lewis/Barcroft Cars; **102** (tr) © tanja-vashchuk/Shutterstock.com, (c) © Viktorija Reuta/Shutterstock.com, (br) © Nuamfolio/Shutterstock.com; **103** (t) © Gino Santa Maria/Shutterstock.com, (c) ACTIVE MUSEUM/Alamy Stock Photo, (b) © MARGRIT HIRSCH/Shutterstock.com; **104–105** REUTERS/Kim Kyung-Hoon; **106–107** © Nor Gal/Shutterstock.com; **108–109** Courtesy of Wildlife SOS; **110** (tr) © Public Domain {{PD-US}}, (cl) © Fun Way Illustration/Shutterstock.com, (c) © Petr Bukal/Shutterstock.com; **112–113** James D. Morgan/REX/Shutterstock; **114** (t) Cleon Daniel/Rex Features, (b) Jonatan Alter; **115** SentIntoSpace.com; **116** (tl) © Peerapong W.Aussawa/Shutterstock.com, (c) © cowardlion/Shutterstock.com, (cr) © MrNovel/Shutterstock.com, (bl) © MrNovel/Shutterstock.com, (br) © MrNovel/Shutterstock.com; **117** (tr) © livcool/Shutterstock.com; **118** (t) © Natalia van D/Shutterstock.com, (bl) Andrew Newman Nature Pictures/Alamy Stock Photo; **119** (tr) © fivespots/Shutterstock.com, (br) blickwinkel/Alamy Stock Photo; **120–121** (t) MattRand/Bournemouth News/REX/Shutterstock; **121** (tr) PA Images/Alamy Stock Photo, (b) Mike Veitch/Alamy Stock Photo; **122–123** (bkg) Devin SuperTramp; **122** (br) © Sferdon/Shutterstock.com, (l) Public Domain {{PD-US}} NASA/http://www.nasa.gov/mission_pages/shuttle/behindscenes/Whatsgoingup.html, (bl) Public Domain {{PD-US}} NASA/https://www.nasa.gov/images/content/194007main_lightsaberpic.jpg; **124** Courtesy of Kayashima Photo Studio Ohana, http://www.studioohana.com/blog/wp-content/uploads/2015/06/%E8%90%B1%E5%B3%B6%E9%A7%8501.jpg; **125** Imaginechina; **126** (t) REUTERS/Mario Anzuoni; **127** (tr) Alex Ramsay/Alamy Stock Photo, (cl) dominic dibbs/Alamy Stock Photo, (cr) Ian Bottle/Alamy Stock Photo, (br) Ian Dagnall/Alamy Stock Photo; **128** (cr) © Rvector/Shutterstock.com; **128–129** dpa picture alliance/Alamy Stock Photo; **129** (br) © SKARIDA/Shutterstock.com; **132–133** Karen Schoeve, Coyote Canyon Farm, Argyle, Texas; **133** (bc) © Cookie Studio/Shutterstock.com, (r) © Jstone/Shutterstock.com; **134** (t) © Debby Wong/Shutterstock.com, (cl, cr) © rvlsoft/Shutterstock.com, (br) © Rob Crandall/Shutterstock.com; **135** (t) © Tidarat Tiemjai/Shutterstock.com, (c) © pixinoo/Shutterstock.com, (br) AF archive/Alamy Stock Photo

**Key:** t = top, b = bottom, c = center, l = left, r = right, sp = single page, bkg = background

All other photos are from Ripley Entertainment Inc.

Every attempt has been made to acknowledge correctly and contact copyright holders, and we apologize in advance for any unintentional errors or omissions, which will be corrected in future editions